WORKBOOK FOR

FOR

WHY I'M NO LONGER TALKING TO WHITE PEOPLE ABOUT RACE

THIS WORKBOOK BELONGS TO

_____

_____

Personal Reflection

_____

_____

_____

_____

_____

_____

_____

How this chapter(s) made me feel	Things on my mind
_____	_____
_____	_____
_____	_____
_____	_____
_____	_____
_____	_____
_____	_____

Lesson Learnt

Lesson from chapter (s)

_____
_____
_____
_____
_____
_____
_____
_____

I am grateful for

_____
_____
_____
_____
_____
_____
_____

Goals I Envision

_____
_____
_____
_____
_____

Improvements I Seek

_____
_____
_____
_____
_____

My Weekly Plan / Meditation

Monday:

_____

_____

Tuesday:

_____

_____

Wednesday:

_____

_____

Thursday:

_____

_____

Friday:

_____

_____

Saturday:

_____

_____

Sunday:

_____

_____

Personal Reflection

_____

_____

_____

_____

_____

_____

_____

_____

How this chapter(s) made me feel

_____

_____

_____

_____

_____

_____

Things on my mind

_____

_____

_____

_____

_____

_____

Lesson Learnt

Lesson from chapter (s)

_____

_____

_____

_____

_____

_____

I am grateful for

_____

_____

_____

_____

_____

_____

Goals I Envision

_____

_____

_____

_____

_____

Improvements I Seek

_____

_____

_____

_____

_____

My Weekly Plan / Meditation

Monday:

_____

_____

Tuesday:

_____

_____

Wednesday:

_____

_____

Thursday:

_____

_____

Friday:

_____

_____

Saturday:

_____

_____

Sunday:

_____

_____

Personal Reflection

_____

_____

_____

_____

_____

_____

_____

How this chapter(s) made me feel

_____

_____

_____

_____

_____

_____

Things on my mind

_____

_____

_____

_____

_____

_____

Lesson Learnt

Lesson from chapter (s)

_____
_____
_____
_____
_____
_____
_____
_____

I am grateful for

_____
_____
_____
_____
_____
_____
_____
_____

Goals I Envision

_____
_____
_____
_____
_____

Improvements I Seek

_____
_____
_____
_____
_____

My Weekly Plan / Meditation

Monday:

_____

Tuesday:

_____

Wednesday:

_____

Thursday:

_____

Friday:

_____

Saturday:

_____

Sunday:

_____

Personal Reflection

_____

_____

_____

_____

_____

_____

_____

_____

How this chapter(s) made me feel

_____

_____

_____

_____

_____

_____

Things on my mind

_____

_____

_____

_____

_____

_____

Lesson Learnt

Lesson from chapter (s)

_____

_____

_____

_____

_____

_____

_____

I am grateful for

_____

_____

_____

_____

_____

_____

Goals I Envision

_____

_____

_____

_____

Improvements I Seek

_____

_____

_____

_____

My Weekly Plan / Meditation

Monday:

_____

_____

Tuesday:

_____

_____

Wednesday:

_____

_____

Thursday:

_____

_____

Friday:

_____

_____

Saturday:

_____

_____

Sunday:

_____

_____

Personal Reflection

_____

_____

_____

_____

_____

_____

_____

How this chapter(s) made me feel

_____

_____

_____

_____

_____

_____

Things on my mind

_____

_____

_____

_____

_____

_____

Lesson Learnt

Lesson from chapter (s)

_____

_____

_____

_____

_____

_____

_____

I am grateful for

_____

_____

_____

_____

_____

Goals I Envision

_____

_____

_____

_____

Improvements I Seek

_____

_____

_____

_____

My Weekly Plan / Meditation

Monday:

_____

_____

Tuesday:

_____

_____

Wednesday:

_____

_____

Thursday:

_____

_____

Friday:

_____

_____

Saturday:

_____

_____

Sunday:

_____

_____

Personal Reflection

_____

_____

_____

_____

_____

_____

_____

_____

How this chapter(s) made me feel	Things on my mind
_____	_____
_____	_____
_____	_____
_____	_____
_____	_____
_____	_____

Lesson Learnt

Lesson from chapter (s)

_____
_____
_____
_____
_____
_____
_____

I am grateful for

_____
_____
_____
_____
_____
_____
_____

Goals I Envision

_____
_____
_____
_____
_____

Improvements I Seek

_____
_____
_____
_____
_____

My Weekly Plan / Meditation

Monday:

_____

_____

Tuesday:

_____

_____

Wednesday:

_____

_____

Thursday:

_____

_____

Friday:

_____

_____

Saturday:

_____

_____

Sunday:

_____

_____

Personal Reflection

_____

_____

_____

_____

_____

_____

_____

How this chapter(s) made me feel	Things on my mind
_____	_____
_____	_____
_____	_____
_____	_____
_____	_____
_____	_____

Lesson Learnt

Lesson from chapter (s)

_____

_____

_____

_____

_____

_____

_____

I am grateful for

_____

_____

_____

_____

_____

_____

_____

Goals I Envision

_____

_____

_____

_____

_____

Improvements I Seek

_____

_____

_____

_____

_____

My Weekly Plan / Meditation

Monday:

_____

_____

Tuesday:

_____

_____

Wednesday:

_____

_____

Thursday:

_____

_____

Friday:

_____

_____

Saturday:

_____

_____

Sunday:

_____

_____

Personal Reflection

_____

_____

_____

_____

_____

_____

_____

_____

How this chapter(s) made me feel

_____

_____

_____

_____

_____

_____

Things on my mind

_____

_____

_____

_____

_____

_____

Lesson Learnt

Lesson from chapter (s)

_____
_____
_____
_____
_____
_____
_____

I am grateful for

_____
_____
_____
_____
_____
_____
_____

Goals I Envision

_____
_____
_____
_____
_____

Improvements I Seek

_____
_____
_____
_____
_____

My Weekly Plan / Meditation

Monday:

_____

_____

Tuesday:

_____

_____

Wednesday:

_____

_____

Thursday:

_____

_____

Friday:

_____

_____

Saturday:

_____

_____

Sunday:

_____

_____

Personal Reflection

_____

_____

_____

_____

_____

_____

_____

_____

How this chapter(s) made me feel

_____

_____

_____

_____

_____

_____

_____

Things on my mind

_____

_____

_____

_____

_____

_____

_____

Lesson Learnt

Lesson from chapter (s)

_____

_____

_____

_____

_____

_____

I am grateful for

_____

_____

_____

_____

_____

_____

Goals I Envision

_____

_____

_____

_____

Improvements I Seek

_____

_____

_____

_____

My Weekly Plan / Meditation

Monday:

_____

_____

Tuesday:

_____

_____

Wednesday:

_____

_____

Thursday:

_____

_____

Friday:

_____

_____

Saturday:

_____

_____

Sunday:

_____

_____

Personal Reflection

_____

_____

_____

_____

_____

_____

_____

_____

How this chapter(s) made me feel

_____

_____

_____

_____

_____

_____

Things on my mind

_____

_____

_____

_____

_____

_____

Lesson Learnt

Lesson from chapter (s)

_____
_____
_____
_____
_____
_____
_____

I am grateful for

_____
_____
_____
_____
_____
_____
_____

Goals I Envision

_____
_____
_____
_____

Improvements I Seek

_____
_____
_____
_____

My Weekly Plan / Meditation

Monday:

_____

_____

Tuesday:

_____

_____

Wednesday:

_____

_____

Thursday:

_____

_____

Friday:

_____

_____

Saturday:

_____

_____

Sunday:

_____

_____

Personal Reflection

_____

_____

_____

_____

_____

_____

_____

_____

How this chapter(s) made me feel

_____

_____

_____

_____

_____

_____

Things on my mind

_____

_____

_____

_____

_____

_____

Lesson Learnt

Lesson from chapter (s)

_____

_____

_____

_____

_____

_____

_____

I am grateful for

_____

_____

_____

_____

_____

_____

_____

Goals I Envision

_____

_____

_____

_____

_____

Improvements I Seek

_____

_____

_____

_____

_____

My Weekly Plan / Meditation

Monday:

_____

_____

Tuesday:

_____

_____

Wednesday:

_____

_____

Thursday:

_____

_____

Friday:

_____

_____

Saturday:

_____

_____

Sunday:

_____

_____

Personal Reflection

_____

_____

_____

_____

_____

_____

_____

_____

How this chapter(s) made me feel	Things on my mind
_____	_____
_____	_____
_____	_____
_____	_____
_____	_____
_____	_____

Lesson Learnt

Lesson from chapter (s)

_____
_____
_____
_____
_____
_____
_____

I am grateful for

_____
_____
_____
_____
_____
_____

Goals I Envision

_____
_____
_____
_____
_____

Improvements I Seek

_____
_____
_____
_____
_____

My Weekly Plan / Meditation

Monday:

_____

_____

Tuesday:

_____

_____

Wednesday:

_____

_____

Thursday:

_____

_____

Friday:

_____

_____

Saturday:

_____

_____

Sunday:

_____

_____

Personal Reflection

_____
_____
_____
_____
_____
_____
_____

How this chapter(s) made me feel

_____
_____
_____
_____
_____
_____
_____

Things on my mind

_____
_____
_____
_____
_____
_____

Lesson Learnt

Lesson from chapter (s)

_____
_____
_____
_____
_____
_____
_____

I am grateful for

_____
_____
_____
_____
_____
_____
_____

Goals I Envision

_____
_____
_____
_____
_____

Improvements I Seek

_____
_____
_____
_____
_____

My Weekly Plan / Meditation

Monday:

_____

Tuesday:

_____

Wednesday:

_____

Thursday:

_____

Friday:

_____

Saturday:

_____

Sunday:

_____

Personal Reflection

_____
_____
_____
_____
_____
_____
_____
_____

How this chapter(s) made me feel

_____
_____
_____
_____
_____
_____

Things on my mind

_____
_____
_____
_____
_____
_____

Lesson Learnt

Lesson from chapter (s)

_____

_____

_____

_____

_____

_____

_____

I am grateful for

_____

_____

_____

_____

_____

_____

_____

Goals I Envision

_____

_____

_____

_____

_____

Improvements I Seek

_____

_____

_____

_____

_____

My Weekly Plan / Meditation

Monday:

_____

_____

Tuesday:

_____

_____

Wednesday:

_____

_____

Thursday:

_____

_____

Friday:

_____

_____

Saturday:

_____

_____

Sunday:

_____

_____

Personal Reflection

_____

_____

_____

_____

_____

_____

_____

_____

How this chapter(s) made me feel

_____

_____

_____

_____

_____

_____

Things on my mind

_____

_____

_____

_____

_____

_____

Lesson Learnt

Lesson from chapter (s)

_____
_____
_____
_____
_____
_____
_____
_____

I am grateful for

_____
_____
_____
_____
_____
_____
_____

Goals I Envision

_____
_____
_____
_____
_____

Improvements I Seek

_____
_____
_____
_____
_____

My Weekly Plan / Meditation

Monday:

_____

_____

Tuesday:

_____

_____

Wednesday:

_____

_____

Thursday:

_____

_____

Friday:

_____

_____

Saturday:

_____

_____

Sunday:

_____

_____

Personal Reflection

_____

_____

_____

_____

_____

_____

_____

_____

How this chapter(s) made me feel

_____

_____

_____

_____

_____

_____

Things on my mind

_____

_____

_____

_____

_____

_____

Lesson Learnt

Lesson from chapter (s)

_____

_____

_____

_____

_____

_____

_____

I am grateful for

_____

_____

_____

_____

_____

_____

Goals I Envision

_____

_____

_____

_____

Improvements I Seek

_____

_____

_____

_____

My Weekly Plan / Meditation

Monday:

_____

Tuesday:

_____

Wednesday:

_____

Thursday:

_____

Friday:

_____

Saturday:

_____

Sunday:

_____

Personal Reflection

_____
_____
_____
_____
_____
_____
_____
_____

How this chapter(s) made me feel

_____
_____
_____
_____
_____
_____

Things on my mind

_____
_____
_____
_____
_____
_____

Lesson Learnt

Lesson from chapter (s)

_____
_____
_____
_____
_____
_____
_____
_____

I am grateful for

_____
_____
_____
_____
_____
_____
_____

Goals I Envision

_____
_____
_____
_____
_____

Improvements I Seek

_____
_____
_____
_____
_____

My Weekly Plan / Meditation

Monday:

_____

Tuesday:

_____

Wednesday:

_____

Thursday:

_____

Friday:

_____

Saturday:

_____

Sunday:

_____

Personal Reflection

_____

_____

_____

_____

_____

_____

_____

_____

How this chapter(s) made me feel	Things on my mind
_____	_____
_____	_____
_____	_____
_____	_____
_____	_____
_____	_____

Lesson Learnt

Lesson from chapter (s)

_____

_____

_____

_____

_____

_____

_____

I am grateful for

_____

_____

_____

_____

_____

_____

_____

Goals I Envision

_____

_____

_____

_____

_____

Improvements I Seek

_____

_____

_____

_____

_____

My Weekly Plan / Meditation

Monday:

_____

_____

Tuesday:

_____

_____

Wednesday:

_____

_____

Thursday:

_____

_____

Friday:

_____

_____

Saturday:

_____

_____

Sunday:

_____

_____

Personal Reflection

_____
_____
_____
_____
_____
_____
_____
_____

How this chapter(s) made me feel

_____
_____
_____
_____
_____
_____
_____

Things on my mind

_____
_____
_____
_____
_____
_____

Lesson Learnt

Lesson from chapter (s)

_____
_____
_____
_____
_____
_____
_____

I am grateful for

_____
_____
_____
_____
_____
_____

Goals I Envision

_____
_____
_____
_____
_____

Improvements I Seek

_____
_____
_____
_____
_____

My Weekly Plan / Meditation

Monday:

_____

_____

Tuesday:

_____

_____

Wednesday:

_____

_____

Thursday:

_____

_____

Friday:

_____

_____

Saturday:

_____

_____

Sunday:

_____

_____

Printed in Great Britain
by Amazon